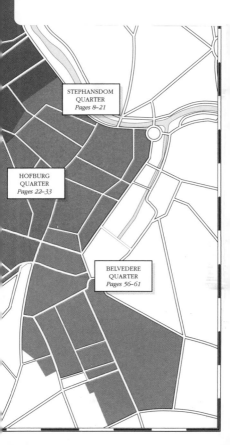

EYEWITNESS TRAVEL

VIENNA

POCKET GUIDE

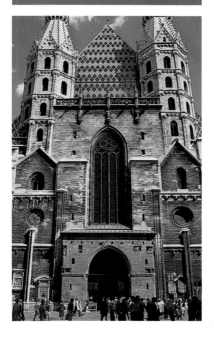

LONDON, NEW YORK,
MELBOURNE, MUNICH AND DELHI
www.dk.com

This edition produced by Silva Editions Ltd.,
233 Woodcote Road, Purley, Surrey CR8 3PB

PROJECT EDITOR Sylvia Goulding

ART EDITOR Paula Keogh

RESEARCH Mike Goulding

CARTOGRAPHER John Plumer

Conceived by Redback Publishing,
25 Longhope Drive, Farnham, Surrey GU10 4SN

Reproduced by Colourscan (Singapore)

Printed and bound in China by Leo Paper Products Ltd

First published in Great Britain in 2007
by Dorling Kindersley Limited
80 Strand, London WC2R 0RL

A CIP CATALOGUE RECORD IS AVAILABLE FROM THE BRITISH LIBRARY.

ISBN 978-1-40531-782-5

**The information in this
DK Eyewitness Travel Guide is checked regularly.**
Every effort has been made to ensure that this book is as up-to-date as
possible at the time of going to press. Some details, however, such as
telephone numbers, opening hours, prices, gallery hanging
arrangements and travel information, are liable to change. The
publishers cannot accept responsibility for any consequences arising
from the use of this book, nor for any material on third-party websites,
and cannot guarantee that any website address in this book will be a
suitable source of travel information. We value the views and
suggestions of our readers highly. Please write to:
Publisher, DK Eyewitness Travel Guides,
Dorling Kindersley, 80 Strand, London WC2R 0RL.

Schloss Schönbrunn, seen from the gardens

CONTENTS

INTRODUCING VIENNA

Johann Strauss statue, Stadtpark

VIENNA AREA BY AREA

PRACTICAL INFORMATION

The giant ferris wheel in the Prater

Central Vienna

This book divides central Vienna into six areas.
Each area chapter contains a collection of sights
that convey some of that area's distinctive
character, such as the imperial buildings in the
Hofburg Quarter. There is a further section
for sights on the outskirts of the city.

Hofburg Complex
*The former imperial palace, with its many
wings and courtyards, has always been of
historical importance. The interior reflects
Austria's glorious past and is the setting
for grand balls (see pp26–7).*

Coffee houses
*Vienna boasts many splendid
coffee houses such as Café
Central (see p37), serving
out-of-this-world cakes
and pastries.*

KEY

Ⓤ	U-Bahn Station
🚋	Badner Bahn stop
ℹ	Tourist information Office

SPITALGASSE

ALSERSTRAS

LAUDONGASSE

LEDERERGASSE

FLORIANI

MUSEU
AND
TOWNH
QUARTE

STROZZIGASSE

LERCHENFELD

NEUSTIF

BURGG

KIRCHENGASSE

SIEBE

MARIAHILFEGASSE

SCHADEKGAS

ESTERHAZY-
PARK

WEBGASSE

STUMPERGASSE

LINIENGASSE

GUMPENDORFER

ESTERHAZYGASSE

REE STRA

WIEN Z

MOLLARDGASSE

LINKE

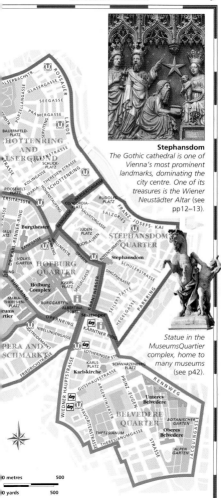

Stephansdom
The Gothic cathedral is one of Vienna's most prominent landmarks, dominating the city centre. One of its treasures is the Wiener Neustädter Altar (see pp12–13).

Statue in the MuseumsQuartier complex, home to many museums (see p42).

0 metres 500

0 yards 500

Vienna's Highlights

Magnificent imperial palaces, imposing churches, as well as splendid historic and modern architecture, all make Vienna a wonderful city to visit, oozing both charm and atmosphere. A brimming cultural scene and vibrant nightlife add to its lasting appeal.

The Palm House in Schloss Schönbrunn (see pp68–9).

Palaces and Gardens

Schloss Schönbrunn
The former summer residence of the imperial Habsburg family is a magnificent palace with Baroque gardens, a superb Palm House and the world's oldest zoo *(see pp68–9)*.

Hofburg Palace
The former imperial palace, with its many wings and courtyards has always been of historic importance. The interior reflects Austria's glorious past *(see pp26–7)*.

Belvedere and Alpengarten
The former summer residence of the 17th-century war hero Prince Eugene, is a splendid Baroque palace with vast French and alpine gardens, and is now home to the Austrian National Gallery *(see p60)*.

Prater
The former imperial hunting grounds are today an expansive park. Within it are a pleasure pavilion, two race courses and the Wurstelprater amusement park with its famous giant ferris wheel *(see p66)*.

Volksgarten
This garden is a popular innercity green space with some beautiful rosebeds and an exhibition space in a replica of Athens' Temple of Theseus *(see p31)*.

Museums and Galleries

MuseumsQuartier
The former imperial stables have been converted into a large museum complex, showcasing, among other things, contemporary and modern art *(see p42)*.

Kunsthistorisches Museum
The Museum of Art History is a world-class gem that should not be missed by any visitor *(see pp46–7)*.

Natural History Museum
The Museum of Natural History's collections include fascinating objects from natural history, geology and archaeology *(see p43)*.

Jüdisches Museum
The history of Vienna's Jews is chronicled at the Jewish museum in Dorotheergasse and its extension

Museumsquartier in the former imperial stables (see p42).

The Wiener Neustädter Altar in Stephansdom (see pp12–13).

on Judenplatz, where you can also see the Holocaust Museum *(see pp19 & 25)*.

Lipizzanermuseum
An exhibition dedicated to the elegant white stallions of the Spanish Riding School *(see p29)*.

Churches

Stephansdom
Vienna's spectacular Gothic cathedral sits at the heart of the city and dominates the skyline *(see pp12–13)*.

Karlskirche
This stunning church combines Oriental and Baroque flourishes. It was built to give thanks for delivery from the plague *(see p58)*.

Votivkirche
The impressive Neo-Gothic church was built in gratitude when Franz Joseph survived an assassination attempt *(see p37)*.

Franziskanerkirche
This church has a Renaissance façade but also bears many Gothic and Baroque features *(see p15)*.

Michaelerkirche
The imperial court attended mass at this church, opposite the Hofburg. Originally Romanesque in style, it was much altered over the centuries *(see p25)*.

Art Nouveau Architecture

Karlsplatz Pavilions
These stunning steel and marble buildings, with gold ornament, were designed by Otto Wagner as underground stations *(see p59)*.

Kaiser Pavilion
Another Otto Wagner-designed station, this is shaped like a white cube with copper ironwork and a copper dome *(see p69)*.

Wagner Apartments
There are two fabulous buildings here, both by Otto Wagner, with glass ornament by Kolo Moser: the superb Majolikahaus and the six-storey house next to it *(see p55)*.

The Secession Building, a superb Art Nouveau structure (see p54).

Secession Building
The simple white Secession building is a magnificent Art Nouveau edifice that reflects the ideals of the movement – purity and functionalism *(see p54)*.

Kirche am Steinhof
Another Art Nouveau gem, this place of worship was designed to bring aesthetic pleasure to psychiatric patients *(see p64)*.

STEPHANSDOM QUARTER

The winding streets and spacious squares of this area form the ancient core of Vienna, and every succeeding age is represented here. Many of the buildings house government offices, businesses, taverns and stylish shops. Dominating them all is the Stephansdom, the focus of the city.

SIGHTS AT A GLANCE

Streets and Squares
Am Hof 25
Annagasse 13
Bäckerstrasse 11
Blutgasse 3
Fleischmarkt 15
Hoher Markt 18
Jewish District 17
Judenplatz 21
Schönlaterngasse 7
Sonnenfelsgasse 9

Historic Buildings
Altes Rathaus 19
Heiligenkreuzerhof 10
Mozarthaus Vienna 4

Churches and Cathedrals
Annakirche 14
Deutschordenskirche 2
Dominikanerkirche 5
Franziskanerkirche 12
Jesuitenkirche 6
Kirche am Hof 24
Maria am Gestade 20
Peterskirche 26
Stephansdom pp12–13 1

Museums and Galleries
Austrian Museum of Applied Arts 16
Cathedral Museum 8
Clock Museum 22
Doll and Toy Museum 23

SEE ALSO

• Street Life p21

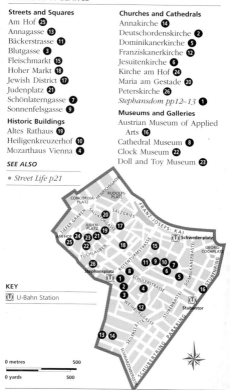

KEY

U U-Bahn Station

| 0 metres | 500 |
| 0 yards | 500 |

◄ Sculpture (1729) in the Peterskirche by Lorenzo Mattielli

Winged altarpiece in the Deutschordenskirche (1520)

Stephansdom ❶

See pp12–13.

Deutschordenskirche ❷

Map E5. Singerstrasse 7. Open daily. Treasury Mon & Wed–Sat. Free.

This church belongs to the Order of Teutonic Knights, a chivalric order which was established in the 12th century. It is 14th-century Gothic, but was restored in the 1720s by Anton Erhard Martinelli. On the walls are numerous coats of arms of teutonic knights. A Flemish altarpiece from 1520 incorporates panel paintings and carvings of scenes from *The Passion* beneath delicate traceried canopies. The Order's Treasury, off the church's courtyard, now serves as a museum. The Grand Masters' collections that are shown here include coins, medals, chalices, maces, daggers and ceremonial items. Also exhibited are some Gothic paintings and a carving of *St George and the Dragon* (1457).

Blutgasse ❸

Map E5.

A local legend relates that this street acquired its gruesome name – Blood Lane – after a massacre in 1312 of the Knights Templar (a military and religious order) in a skirmish so violent that the streets flowed with blood. But there is no evidence to support this story and the street's name belies its charm. Its tall apartment buildings, dating mostly from the 18th century, have been impressively restored. The buildings and their courtyards are now linked; No. 9, known as Fähnrichshof, is particularly attractive.

Inner courtyard of No. 9 Blutgasse, the Fähnrichshof

Mozarthaus Vienna ❹

Map E5. Domgasse 5. Open daily. Adm charge.

Mozart and his family occupied a flat on the first floor of this house in 1784–87. Of Mozart's 11 Viennese residences, this is the one where he is said to have been happiest, and where he composed some of his masterworks: the exquisite Haydn quartets, a handful of piano concerti, and *The Marriage of Figaro*. Restored for the anniversary year 2006, the Mozarthaus now has exhibitions on two upper floors as well as the Mozarts' first-floor flat.

Pulpit detail in the Jesuitenkirche

Dominikanerkirche ❺

Map E6. Postgasse 4. Open daily. Free.

The Dominican order of monks came to Vienna in 1226, and by 1237 they had consecrated a church. In the 1630s, Antonio Canecale designed their present church, which boasts a majestic and really rather handsome Baroque façade. The interior is equally imposing. The central chapel on the right has swirling Rococo grilles and candelabra. Also worth seeing is the superb gilt organ above the west door, its casing dating from the mid-18th century. The frescoes by Tencala and Rauchmiller are especially noteworthy, as is the high altar.

Jesuitenkirche ❻

Map E6. Dr-Ignaz-Seipel-Platz 1. Open daily. Free.

This church, built in the early 1600s, dominates the square with its broad, high façade. In the 1620s the Jesuits decided to move their headquarters here in order to be near the Old University, which they controlled. The Jesuits were the dominant force behind the Counter-Reformation, and not afraid to make a statement. The grandeur of this church reflects their dominance. Emperor Leopold I commissioned the Italian architect Andrea Pozzo to design the magnificent frescoes and paintings. Pozzo also painted the barrel-vaulted ceiling with a *trompe l'oeil*, which gives the illusion of a dome. The pews are richly carved.

Nave of the Dominikanerkirche

Stephansdom ❶

The "Steffl", as it is lovingly known, is situated in the heart of Vienna. Little remains of the original church, dating back to 1147; the Gothic nave, choir and side chapels all hail from the 14th and 15th centuries. After damage in World War II the Dom was rebuilt as a symbol of hope.

The North Tower, with the green cupola, houses the "Pummerin", a 20-ton bell cast from 100 cannon balls seized during the Turkish siege of Vienna in 1683.

Carving of Rudolf IV

Main entrance

The Singer Gate, once the entrance for male visitors, has a sculpted relief with scenes from the life of St Paul.

The Gargoyles
on the roof of the cathedral are cast in the shape of dragons and other mythical animals.

The Big Spire or Steffl

The Tiled Roof is covered with almost 250,000 colourful glazed tiles, laid out as the Habsburg coat of arms.

The High Altar
was created by the brothers Tobias and Johann Pock in 1641. The painting in the centre depicts the stoning of St Stephen.

South-eastern entrance

Lower vestry

Pilgram's Pulpit

VISITORS' CHECKLIST

Map E5. Stephansplatz. Tel 01 515 523 526. Open 6am–10pm daily. Guided tours 10.30am & 3pm Mon–Sat, 3pm Sun. Adm charge for North and South Towers. www.stephansdom.at

Schönlaterngasse, named after this attractive lantern

Schönlaterngasse ❼

Map D6.

This attractive, curving lane is named after the wrought-iron lantern outside No. 6, a copy of the 1610 original. No. 4 dates from the early 17th century, while No. 7, the Basiliskenhaus, is of medieval origin. It displays on its façade an artist's impression, dating from 1740, of a mythical serpent said to have been found in a well by the house in 1212. No. 7a was the home of the composer Robert Schumann (1838–39). A large smithy has been reassembled at No. 9, which also contains halls for cultural events.

Cathedral Museum ❽

Map E5. Stephansplatz 6. Open Tue–Sat except 24 & 31 Dec, Maundy Thu & Easter Mon. Adm charge.

The Erzbischöfliches Dom- und Diözesanmuseum contains some important medieval carvings of the Madonna and Child and spectacular items from Duke Rudolf IV's personal collection, including a portrait of him by a Bohemian master dating from the 1360s. His shroud and the St Leopold reliquary (1592) are also housed here.

Sonnenfelsgasse ❾

Map D5–6.

Attractive houses line this pleasant street, named after a soldier and legal advisor of Maria Theresa. Under his guidance, she reformed the penal code and abolished torture. On the north side are solid merchant and patrician houses dating from the late 1700s. No. 19, built in 1628 and renovated in 1721, was once part of the Old University. No. 11 has an impressive courtyard. Here many balconies have been glassed in to provide additional living space. The Zwölf Apostelkeller at No. 3 is a city wine growers' inn; note its elaborate façade.

Portrait of Duke Rudolph IV

Heiligenkreuzerhof

Map D6. Schönlaterngasse 5. Open Mon–Sat. Free.

Founded by the abbey of Heiligenkreuz as a city monastery in the Middle Ages, the buildings around the courtyard today house Vienna's Applied Arts College. On the south side is the Bernhardskapelle, a Baroque chapel dating from 1662, but altered in the 1730s.

Bäckerstrasse

Map D5–E6.

This street used to house the city's bakers in medieval times, but today it is better known for its nightlife. At No. 1 is the site of the Alter Regensburgerhof, where Bavarian merchants received incentives to work in Vienna. Opposite, No. 2 boasts a 17th-century tower and an attractive courtyard. No. 8 is the former home and palace of Count Seilern, dating from 1722, and No. 7 is known for its arcaded courtyard and stables in Renaissance style. There are two more Renaissance houses at Nos. 12 and 14.

Detail from Andrea Pozzo's Baroque altar (1707) in Franziskanerkirche

Franziskanerkirche

Map E5. Franziskanerplatz 4. Open daily. Free.

Located on the charming Franziskanerplatz, this church, of the Franciscan Order, was built in 1603–11, on the site of a former medieval convent. Its façade is in South German Renaissance style, and is topped by an elaborate scrolled gable with obelisks. The interior, however, is full-blown Baroque. It features a fine pulpit from 1726, richly carved pews and a dramatic, high altar by Andrea Pozzo. Only its front part is three-dimensional, the rest is *trompe l'oeil*.

A fresco on the Renaissance building at No. 12 Bäckerstrasse

Annagasse ⑬

Map F5.

Now splendidly Baroque, pedestrianized Annagasse dates from medieval times. Of note are the luxurious Mailberger Hof and the stucco-decorated Römischer Kaiser hotels. No. 14's lintel has a Baroque carving of babes making merry, while above this is a relief of the blue carp that gives this former pub its name: Zum Blauen Karpfen. No. 2 is the 17th-century Esterházy Palace, now a casino.

Annakirche ⑭

Map E5. Annagasse 3b. Open daily. Free.

There has been a chapel in Annagasse since 1320, but the present church dates from 1629–34; in the 18th century it was renovated. Its finest exterior feature is the copper cupola. Inside, on the high altar, is a richly coloured painting of St Anne by Daniel Gran, a leading

Moulded copper cupola over the tower of the Annakirche

painter of the Austrian Baroque period. Ceiling frescoes, also by Gran, are now fading. The first chapel on the left houses a copy of a carving of St Anne from about 1505 – the original is in the Cathedral Museum *(see p14)*. St Anne is portrayed as a powerful mother figure, with her daughter, the Virgin Mary, who in turn holds the baby Jesus. This saint is deeply revered in Vienna, and the intimate Annakirche is often full of quiet worshippers.

Fleischmarkt ⑮

Map D6.

In Fleischmarkt, the former meat market dating back to 1220, stands the Griechen-beisl, one of Vienna's oldest inns. It is graced by Mozart's signature. On its façade is a woodcarving of "Dear Old Augustin", who is said to have escaped being buried in a plague pit in 1679 by playing his bagpipe.

Carving of the bagpiper on a façade in Fleischmarkt

Austrian Museum of Applied Arts 16

Map E6. Stubenring 5.
Open Tue–Sun, except 1 Jan,
1 May, 1 Nov, 25 Dec. Adm
charge.

The MAK (Museum für Ange-
wandte Kunst) holds one of
Vienna's most exciting and
dynamic collections. First
opened in 1871 as a museum
for art and industry, the MAK
expanded and diversified
over the years to include
objects representing new
artistic movements. Its
exhibits are
arranged by
style, repre-
senting periods
from the Gothic
to the present.

Furniture

The museum
holds furniture
made through
the ages, in an amazing
variety of shapes, designs
and materials. Among the
highlights are some wonderful Empire-style Biedermeier
(1815 to 1848) pieces, including settees, ladies' desks and
cabinets, often made from
cherrywood. World-famous
exhibits are the bentwood

*Cherrywood Biedermeier desk
(c. 1825) of Archduchess Sophie*

chairs by Michael Thonet
(1796–1871), which became
known as Vienna chairs.

Porcelain

Among the MAK's porcelain
exhibits are many excellent
pieces by the Viennese
Porcelain Manufactory. The
Dubsky Porcelain Room
(1724) was recreated from
the Dubsky Palace at Brno,
Czech Republic.

Wiener Werkstätte

The Wiener Werkstätte
arts and crafts cooperative
studio, founded
by Josef Hoff-
man and Kolo
Moser and
active from 1870
to 1956, created
new designs in
architecture,
cabinetmaking,
bookbinding,
metal and
leatherwork, as well as for
fabrics and wallpapers.
At first purely geometric,
the movement's style later
evolved into a highly decorative one. Since 1937, the
MAK has housed the Werk-
stätte archives which include
sketches, fabric patterns and
many fine pieces.

*Wallpaper design Tausendblumen, by Wiener Werkstätte member
Dagobert Peche (1922)*

The interior of the Stadttempel

Jewish District ⑰

Map D5.

Vienna's Jewish district is more famous today for its bars and clubs than for its Jewish community. Vienna's oldest surviving synagogue, the Stadttempel, designed in the 1820s by the Biedermeier architect Josef Kornhäusel, is on Seitenstettengasse. On the same street is the headquarters of Vienna's Jewish community. It used to house the Jewish museum, which is now located in Dorotheergasse *(see p25)*. On Fleischmarkt stands the sombre Kornhäuselturm, a tower built by Kornhäusel, supposedly as a refuge from his wife! In Sterngasse is the Neustädter Hof, a Baroque palace built by Anton Ospel in 1734. A Turkish cannonball, fired in 1683, is embedded in its façade.

Ironwork at the Rathaus entrance

Hoher Markt ⑱

Map D5.

This square is Vienna's oldest, used in medieval times for markets and executions. Here stands the Josefsbrunnen, designed by Johann Bernhard Fischer von Erlach and built by his son Joseph Emanuel in 1729–32. It celebrates the betrothal of Joseph and Mary. Also worth seeing is the Anker Clock, dating from 1914, with its parade of historical figures to organ music.

The Anker Clock in Hoher Markt

Altes Rathaus ⑲

Map D5. Wipplinger Strasse 8. Open Mon, Wed, Sat or by appointment. Free.

The Habsburgs confiscated this palace in 1316 from Otto and Haymo of Neuburg who had conspired against them. It was the town hall until 1883 but is now occupied by shops, offices and the Austrian Resistance Archive on the first floor, where the Austrian resistance to Nazism is documented.

The Holocaust memorial on Judenplatz

Maria am Gestade ⑳

Map D5. Salvatorgasse 12.
Open daily; inside at rear by
appointment only. Free.

This Gothic church boasts
a 56-m (180-ft) high steeple
and immense choir windows.
Dating from the late 1300s,
it was used as an arsenal by
Napoleon's troops in 1809.
The windows behind the
high altar contain fragments
of medieval stained glass.
The choir holds three High
Gothic panels (1460), and
the nave piers are enlivened
with statues from different
eras under Gothic canopies.

*Gothic canopies in the Maria am
Gestade church*

Judenplatz ㉑

Map D5. Museum Judenplatz:
open Sun–Fri except on main
Jewish holidays. Adm charge. Free
2pm & 5pm Thu & Sun. Take ID.

Judenplatz, the site of the
Jewish ghetto in medieval
times, was reopened in 2000
as a place of remembrance.
The Holocaust memorial,
designed by British artist
Rachel Whiteread, commem-
orates the 65,000 Austrian
Jewish victims of the Nazi
regime. Also in the square
are a new Jewish Museum at
No. 8, the reinstated statue of
German playwright Ephraim
Lessing, and the recently
excavated remains of a
medieval synagogue.

Clock Museum ㉒

Map D5. Schulhof 2.
Open Tue–Sun, except 1 Jan,
1 May, 25 Dec. Adm charge.

The Uhrenmuseum in the
beautiful former Obizzi
Palace (1690) contains more
than 3,000 clocks, including
fascinating painted clocks,
the mechanisms of tower
clocks, grandfather clocks
and pocket watches, as well
as huge astronomical clocks
and novelty ones.

A doll's house (about 1920) from the Doll and Toy Museum

Doll and Toy Museum ㉓

Map D5. Schulhof 2. Open Tue–Sun except 1 Jan, 1 May, 25 Dec. Adm charge.

One of Vienna's unusual gems, the Puppen-und Spielzeugmuseum is housed in a fine Baroque building. Originally private, it was opened to the public in 1989 and comprises dolls and toys from the past 200 years. Particularly intriguing are the early 20th-century "exotic" dolls, or South Sea babies; they are black, Polynesian and Oriental models. Also on show are some very opulent dolls' houses from the early 1900s, and some teddy bears.

Kirche am Hof ㉔

Map D5. Open daily. Free.

This fascinating church, dedicated to the Nine Choirs of Angels, was founded by Carmelite friars in the late 14th century. Its façade was redesigned by the Italian architect Carlo Carlone in 1662 to provide space for a large balustraded balcony. It unites, in its architecture, numerous different styles. The church is now used by the Croatian community.

Am Hof ㉕

Map D4.

A large square, dating back to Roman times, today surrounded by mansions, such as Märklinsches Haus, designed by Johann Lukas von Hildebrandt in 1727. The citizens' armoury was at No. 10, now the home of the fire services. Its façade bears the Habsburg coat of arms and military emblems. On top are allegorical statues by Lorenzo Mattielli. At the Collalto Palace the young Mozart made his first public appearance in 1762, aged just six years.

Statues on top of No. 10 Am Hof

Peterskirche ㉖

Map D5. Petersplatz 6. Open daily. Free.

Modelled on St Peter's in Rome, the present church was built to the design of Gabriele Montani and others in the early 18th century. The interior is lavish, with an exuberant pulpit (1716) by Matthias Steindl. The richly clothed skeletons, on the right and beneath the altar, are the remains of early Christian martyrs.

STREET LIFE

RESTAURANTS

Zwölf-Apostelkeller
Map D5. Sonnenfelsgasse 3.
Tel 01 512 6777.
Cheap
Baroque and medieval cellars under the catacombs. Plates of cold cuts and specialities are served with great wines.

Kern's Beisl
Map D5. Kleeblattgasse 4.
Tel 01 533 9188.
Cheap
Busy friendly Beisl (snack bar) serving Viennese and regional Austrian dishes; superb value.

Figlmüller
Map D5. Wollzeile 5.
Tel 01 512 6177.
Moderate
Traditional Viennese eatery famous for its larger-than-plate-sized Schnitzels.

Österreicher im MAK
Map E6. Stubenring 5.
Tel 01 711 36 294 .
Moderate
Top-level modern Viennese cooking by celebrity chef Helmut Österreicher at moderate prices.

Do & Co im Haas Haus
Map E5. Stephansplatz 12.
Tel 01 535 3969.
Expensive
Very stylish restaurant with Vienna's most sought-after view of the Stephansdom.

Zum Schwarzen Kameel
Map D4–D5. Bognergasse 5.
Tel 01 533 8125.
Expensive
Premium Viennese cuisine in superb Art Nouveau restaurant dating back to 1618.

BARS

Ma Pitom
Map D5. Seitenstettengasse 5.
Cosy beer hall and cocktail bar serving international and Austrian dishes to live music.

Onyx Bar
Map E5. Haas Haus, Stephansplatz 12, 7th floor.
Snacks, cocktails and groovy music, as well as great views of the cathedral, draw a trendy crowd of locals and visitors.

COFFEE HOUSES

Café Diglas
Map D5. Wollzeile 10.
A very charming, traditional café with stuccoed walls, serving mouth-watering cakes and pastries made on the premises.

Konditorei Heiner
Map D5. Wollzeile 9.
Once Emperor Franz Joseph's court patisserie, this neo-Biedermeier café is truly enchanting. As well as delicious cakes and pastries, hot desserts and diabetic sweets are on offer.

SHOPPING

Haas & Haas
Map E5. Stephansplatz 4.
This shop offers more than 200 assorted fruit, black and herbal teas, and their marzipan confectionary and chocolates are divine.

MAK Design Shop
Map E6. Stubenring 5.
Museum shop with attractive gifts based in Viennese arts and crafts designs.

See p80 for price codes.

HOFBURG QUARTER

Most of the palaces in the Hofburg area are now offices or embassies. Yet the district remains the most fashionable in Vienna, crammed with coffee houses, elegant shops and art galleries as well as museums and churches.

SIGHTS AT A GLANCE

Streets and Squares
Bankgasse ⑲
Dorotheergasse ⑥
Kärntner Strasse ㉔
Kohlmarkt ⑦
Michaelerplatz ①
Minoritenplatz ⑱
Naglergasse ⑧
Neuer Markt ㉓

Churches and Cathedrals
Augustinerkirche ⑫
Burgkapelle ⑬
Kapuzinerkirche and Kaisergruft ㉒
Michaelerkirche ④
Minoritenkirche ⑰

Parks and Gardens
Volksgarten ⑳

Historic Buildings
Bundeskanzleramt ⑯
Grosses und Kleines Michaelerhaus ③
Hofburg Complex ⑨
Lobkowitz Palace ㉑
Loos Haus ②
Stallburg ⑤
State Apartments and Treasuries ⑮
Winter Riding School ⑭

Museums and Galleries
Albertina ⑪
Völkerkundemuseum ⑩

SEE ALSO

• Street Life p33

KEY

🅄 U-Bahn Station

| 0 metres | 300 |
| 0 yards | 300 |

◀ Detail of the Danubius fountain (1869), outside the Albertina

Michaelerplatz ❶

Map E4.

This square faces the grandiose entrance into the Hofburg, the majestic, semicircular Michaeler Gate. Opposite are the Michaeler-kirche and Loos Haus. On one side of Michaelerplatz stands the Michaelertrakt, commissioned by Franz Joseph in 1888. An earlier design, by Joseph Emanuel Fischer von Erlach, was used as the basis for a new design by Ferdinand Kirschner. It was completed in 1893, with gilt-tasselled cupolas and statues representing Austria's land and sea power.

Loos Haus ❷

Map E4. Michaelerplatz 3. Open Mon–Fri. Free.

Constructed in 1910–12, to designs by Adolf Loos, this building with the emperor and city council with its plain functionality. Loos placated them by adding bronze window-boxes. The interior is a lesson in stylish elegance and not at all plain.

Michaelerplatz fountain

Grosses und Kleines Michaelerhaus ❸

Map E4. Kohlmarkt 11 & Michaelerplatz 6. Closed to the public.

A footpath leads to Kleines Michaelerhaus (1735). Look out for a vivid painted relief of *Christ on the Mount of Olives* with a crucifixion in the background (1494). The Baroque Grosses Michaeler-haus has a handsome court-yard and a coach house. Joseph Haydn is said to have lived in an unheated attic here in 1749.

The controversially plain Loos Haus, on Michaelerplatz

The richly carved Baroque organ (1714) in the Michaelerkirche

Michaelerkirche ❹

Map E4. Michaelerplatz 1. Open daily. Guided tours in summer. Adm charge.

The Michaelerkirche, once the parish church of the court, dates back in part to the 13th century, the choir to 1327–40. Its Neo-Classical façade has Baroque statues (1725) by Lorenzo Mattielli. Inside are Renaissance and 14th-century frescoes, and a glorious organ from 1714 by Johann David Sieber. The main choir (1782), replete with tumbling cherubs and sunbursts, is by Karl Georg Merville. The altarpiece of the north choir (1755) is by Franz Anton Maulbertsch.

Antique jewellery in Dorotheergasse

Stallburg ❺

Map E4. Reitschulgasse 2. Lippizaner Museum open daily. Adm charge.

The Stallburg, built in the mid-16th century for Archduke Maximilian as a royal residence, was later converted to stables for the Hofburg, ranged around a large courtyard with arcades on three storeys. The Stallburg today houses the Spanish Riding School *(see p29)* and the Lipizzaner Museum, which contains exhibits on the history of the horses.

Dorotheergasse ❻

Map E5.

At No. 11 of this street is the Eskeles Palace, now home to the Jewish Museum which, along with its new extension in Judenplatz *(see p19)*, chronicles the city's rich Jewish heritage. Halfway along is the Evangelical church (1783–4), originally by Gottlieb Nigelli. The 17th-century Dorotheum, a pawn-brokers and an auction house with branches all over Vienna, is at No. 27. Head for Dorotheergasse if you are interested in antiques.

The strikingly abstract exterior of the jewellers Schullin in Kohlmarkt

Kohlmarkt **7**

Map E4.

The pedestrianized Kohl-markt, which leads directly up to the Hofburg Palace, is lined with some of Vienna's most exclusive shops and amazing shopfronts. No. 9, the Jugendstil Artaria Haus (1901), was the work of Max Fabiani (1865–1962), a pro-tégé of Otto Wagner. No. 16, the bookshop Manz, boasts an Adolf Loos portal from 1912. The jewellers, Schullin, have a shopfront designed by Hans Hollein (1982).

Naglergasse **8**

Map D4.

This narrow lane was named after the nail-makers who had their shops here in the Middle Ages. Following the line of a Roman wall, it boasts fine Baroque houses, such as No. 19 with its carved cherubs.

The Hofburg Complex **9**

Map E4. Michaelerplatz 1. Open daily. Adm charge.

The Hofburg was the seat of Austrian power for over six centuries, and successive rulers left their mark on the style of the 10 or so build-ings, ranging from Gothic to late 19th-century historicism. Today the palace houses the Albertina *(see p28)*, a church and a chapel *(see p28)*, the Winter Riding School *(see p29)*, the former imperial apartments *(see p29)*, several more museums, the National Library and the offices of the President of Austria.

Austrian National Library

The majestic Burgtor, with a statue of Prince Eugen (1865)

The Gates

A number of gates lead into the palace. The Burgtor is the main entrance and the grandest gate. The Renaissance Schweizertor has red-and-black marble columns and gold inscriptions. Named after Maria Theresa's 18th-century Swiss guards, it leads to the Hofburg's oldest part, the Schweizerhof. The Michaeler Tor, a majestic semi-circular gate with an imposing copper dome, looms over Michaelerplatz.

National Library

Built by Von Erlach, from 1723 to 1726,

The dome above the Michaeler Gate (1893)

this Baroque library is one of the world's finest. Its showpiece is the stunning, wood-panelled Prunksaal, or palatial hall, which features grand marble columns and ceiling frescoes by the Austrian Baroque artist Daniel Gran (1730). The library holds 2.6 million books and many invaluable historic manuscripts.

Völkerkundemuseum ❿

Map E4. Neue Burg – Heldenplatz. Reopens 2007. Adm charge.

Ranged around an arcaded Italian-Renaissance-style courtyard at the west end of the Neue Burg is Vienna's ethnological museum. To one side are the Oriental collections: lacquer screens, clothes, furniture, farm tools, weapons, masks, ceramics and musical instruments. In a neighbouring room are African figurines and masks. The artefacts from Benin are the highlight of the African collection.

Items from Australasia and Polynesia dominate the displays upstairs, with fabrics from Bali, weapons from Borneo and many musical instruments from the Far East. The pre-Columbian collection from Mexico includes an Aztec feather headdress. A recent addition to the collection is a section on Inuit culture.

Façade of the Albertina

Albertina ⓫

Map E4. Augustinerstrasse 1.
Open daily. Adm charge.

The Albertina is a distinctive landmark, its raised entrance boasting a controversial free-standing diving-board roof by architect Hans Hollein. A major renovation and extension restored a number of features, including the façades and the courtyard. The Habsburg State Rooms are now open to the public, for the first time in 200 years.

The palace once belonged to Maria Theresa's daughter, Maria Christina, and her husband Duke Albert of Sachsen-Teschen, after whom the gallery is named. Today the Albertina houses a collection of one million prints, over 65,000 water-colours and drawings, and some 70,000 photographs. The gems of the collections are by Albrecht Dürer, with Michelangelo and Peter Paul Rubens well represented. Pablo Picasso has a fine 20th-century section, which also includes some works by Gustav Klimt.

There is no permanent exhibition, but three halls house the Albertina's annual temporary exhibitions, with regular displays of works from the home collection together with paintings, drawings and prints on loan.

Augustinerkirche ⓬

Map E4. Augustinerstrasse 3.
Open daily.

Built in 1327, the Augustin church has one of the best-preserved 14th-century Gothic interiors in Vienna. Famous as a repository for the hearts of the Habsburgs, it was the wedding chapel for Napoleon and Marie Louise, and for Sisi and Franz Joseph I. The church is also celebrated for its musical Schubert or Haydn masses.

Gothic statue (about 1400) of Leopold III in the Burgkapelle

Burgkapelle ⓭

Map E4. Wiener Hofburg, Schweizerhof. Open Mon–Fri except 1 Nov, 8 Dec, 1 Jan. Adm charge.

From Schweizerhof, steps lead to the Hofburg Chapel, constructed in 1296 but modified 150 years later on the orders of Friedrich III. On Sundays, visitors can hear the Vienna Boys' Choir. Inside, there are Gothic statues in canopied niches, Gothic carvings and a bronze crucifix (1720) by Johann Känischbauer.

Winter Riding School ⑭

Map E4. Michaelerplatz 1. Open for performances, but closed on public holidays.

The Spanish Riding School is believed to have been founded in 1572 to cultivate the classic skills of *haute école* horsemanship. The Habsburgs formed the Spanische Reitschule, training horses from Spain. Commissioned by Karl VI, the Winter Reitschule was built in 1729–35 to a design by Josef Emanuel Fischer von Erlach. Today, 80-minute shows take place here. The famous Lipizzaner horses take their name from the Slovenian stud farm at Lipizza, where they were bred by crossing Spanish, Berber and Arab horses. They are now bred at the national stud near Graz.

A Lipizzaner stallion

State Apartments and Treasuries ⑮

Map E4. Michaelerkuppel. Open daily. Adm charge.

The state apartments of Emperor Franz Joseph and his wife Empress Elisabeth,

and the rooms occupied by Tsar Alexander I during the Congress of Vienna (1815), are open to the public as Schauräume. The sacred and secular treasures of the Habsburgs, including the crown jewels and relics of the Holy Roman Empire, are on show in the Schatzkammer.

One section, the Sisi-Museum, is dedicated to the beautiful and tragic Empress Elisabeth. It chronicles her private life and her rebellion against court ceremony up to her assassination in 1898.

Inside the State Apartments

The Bundeskanzleramt

Bundeskanzleramt 16

Map E4. Ballhausplatz 2. Not open to the public.

The Bundeskanzleramt, or Austrian Chancellery, (1717–19) was designed by Johann Lukas von Hildebrandt. It was expanded to its present size in 1766 by Nikolaus Pacassi. The Foreign Ministry was also based here until the declaration of the Republic in 1918. Major events that shaped Austria's history have taken place here, including several meetings of the Congress of Vienna in 1814–15, the final deliberations in 1914 that led to the outbreak of World War I, and the murder of Chancellor Dollfuss by Nazis in 1934.

No. 4 Minoritenplatz

Minoritenkirche 17

Map D4. Minoritenplatz 2. Open daily. Free.

When Duke Leopold VI returned safely from a crusade in 1219, he built a church on this site. Despite some alterations, its medieval character is still visible. The tower received its odd pyramidal shape during the Turkish siege of 1529, when shells sliced the top off the steeple. In the 1780s the church was restored to its original Gothic style. There is a fine west portal (1340) with statues beneath traceried canopies. The bright and large interior has a mosaic copy of Leonardo da Vinci's *Last Supper* by Giacomo Raffaelli. It was commissioned by Napoleon who intended to leave it in Milan while taking the original to Paris. After his downfall, the Habsburgs bought the copy. In the south aisle is a statue of the Madonna and Child (c1350); in the north aisle part of a 16th-century fresco of St Francis of Assisi.

Minoritenplatz 18

Map D4.

There are several palaces around this square. No. 3 is the former Dietrichstein Palace of 1755. No. 4 is the side of the Liechtenstein Palace. At No. 5 is the mid-17th-century Starhemberg Palace, the former home of Count Starhemberg, a hero of the 1683 Turkish siege. The Baroque-style building (1902) at No. 1 houses the State Archives, an important resource for research.

Fountain in front of the formal rose gardens in the Volksgarten

Bankgasse

Map D4.

Few streets in Vienna are more crammed with the palaces of the nobility. At Nos. 4–6 is the former Strattmann-Windischgrätz Palace (1692–1734), originally designed by Johann Bernhard Fischer von Erlach. The present façade (1783–4) is by Franz Hillebrand, who expanded the building by incorporating the palace next door. Today, it is the home of the Hungarian Embassy. Nos. 5–7 are the back of the Starhemberg Palace. No. 9 is the Liechtenstein Palace, built as a town residence for the Liechtenstein family by Domenico Martinelli (1694–1706). It now also houses a museum. No. 2 is the Baroque Schönborn-Batthyány Palace (1695).

Volksgarten

Map E3. Dr-Karl-Renner-Ring. Open daily. Free.

The Volksgarten was created after the destruction of the city walls by Napoleon. It was opened to the public soon after the garden's completion in 1820. The formal plantations, especially the splendid rose gardens, are matched in grandeur by the garden's ornaments. The Temple of Theseus (1823) by Peter von Nobile was built to house Canova's statue of the Greek hero, which now graces the staircase of the Kunsthistorisches Museum. Other monuments include Karl von Hasenauer's to the poet Franz Grillparzer, and the fountain memorial to the assassinated Empress Elisabeth (1907) by Friedrich Ohmann and the sculptor Hans Bitterlich.

Statuary above the portal to the Lobkowitz Palace

Lobkowitz Palace ㉑

Map E5. Lobkowitzplatz 2. Open Tue–Sun. Adm charge.

The Lobkowitz family's large palace was built 1685–7 by Giovanni Pietro Tencala and altered by Johann Bernhard Fischer von Erlach in 1710. Balls were held here during the Congress of Vienna. Since 1991 it has been the Austrian Theatre Museum, which houses a model of the first Hofburg theatre and the Eroica-Saal (1724–29), where much of Beethoven's work was first performed.

Kapuzinerkirche und Kaisergruft ㉒

Map E5. Tegetthoffstrasse 2. Open daily. Adm charge.

The crypt beneath the Kapuzinerkirche was established by Empress Anna in 1618 and served as the Habsburgs' burial place for more than 350 years. Among the 146 bodies resting here are those of Maria Theresa and her husband Franz Stephan in a tomb by Balthasar Moll (1753). The most poignant is that of Franz Joseph, next to his assassinated wife Elisabeth and their son Rudolf.

Neuer Markt ㉓

Map E5.

Known as the Mehlmarkt or flour market until around 1210, the Neuer Markt was also used as a jousting area. Of these origins nothing is left, though a few 18th-century houses remain. In the middle of the Neuer Markt is a replica of the Donner Fountain (1737–9) by Georg Raphael Donner, a symbolic celebration of the role played by rivers in the economic life of the Habsburg Empire. The four figures denote tributaries of the Danube, while the central figure represents Providence. The original figures are in the Lower Belvedere *(see pp60–61)*.

Kärntner Strasse ㉔

Map E5.

This pedestrianized street, once the main highway to Kärnten (Carinthia), is now one of the city's principal shopping streets, packed day and night with people shopping, pausing in cafés, or listening to the buskers. No. 37 is the Malteserkirche, founded by the Knights of Malta who came to Vienna early in the 13th century. The interior retains lofty Gothic windows and vaults. At No. 1 is the Lobmeyr Museum. It exhibits glass designed by Josef Hoffmann and others. Nearby, at No. 5 Johannesgasse, is the grand 18th-century Questenberg-Kaunitz Palace.

Tomb of Karl VI by Balthasar Moll

STREET LIFE

RESTAURANTS

Ilona Stüberl
Map E5. Bräunerstrasse 2.
Tel 01 533 9029.
Cheap
Massive helpings of traditional Hungarian fare, like stuffed cabbage, paprika chicken and goulash, at reasonable prices. Pleasant area to sit outside on a pedestrian-only street.

Palmenhaus im Burggarten
Map E4. Burggarten/ Albertina Entrance.
Tel 01 533 1033.
Medium
Mediterranean-style food, served in the delightful Art Nouveau palm conservatory, next to the Butterfly House in the Burggarten. Dishes are prepared with seasonal produce, and there's an impressive wine list, including many Austrian wines. In summer there is a bar outside.

Novelli Bacaro con Cucina
Map E5. Bräunerstrasse 11.
Tel 01 513 4200.
Expensive
Fine Italian restaurant located in the Palais Pallavicini. Classic cooking with homemade pasta and an excellent wine list. The colourful conversion of the palace interior will delight the diner's eye.

BARS AND PUBS

American Bar
Map E5. Kärntner Strasse 10.
Small bar in a simple but sophisticated Adolf Loos-designed interior. One of the most beautiful nightspots in town, it also serves a large number of great cocktails.

COFFEE HOUSES

Demel Konditorei
Map E4. Kohlmarkt 14.
Vienna's most refined retreat for cake-lovers, the famous "royal & imperial" confectioners offers a light lunch and a huge selection of pastries served in an elegant Neo-Classical interior. Empress Sisi loved the Demel violet sorbet.

Café Hawelka
Map E5. Dorotheergasse 6.
A Viennese institution, the preferred café of the city's Bohemians and their dogs. Spartan interior, breakfast until 11am, and Buchteln (warm yeast buns filled with jam) after 10pm.

SHOPPING

Loden Plankl
Map E4. Michaelerplatz 6.
Traditional Austrian clothing ranging from Loden coats and jackets to beautiful Dirndl dresses and Lederhosen. Also stocks modern versions of traditional garments.

Doblinger
Map E5. Dorotheergasse 10.
Excellent choice if you're looking for sheet music; it also has a second-hand department and a CD shop.

J & L Lobmeyr
Map E5. Kärntner Strasse 26.
The suppliers of chandeliers at Vienna's Opera House and the Metropolitan Opera in New York. Sells crystal chandeliers and glasses, including the very fine Musselinglass. Has a small museum on the first floor.

See p80 for price codes.

SCHOTTENRING AND ALSERGRUND

Apart from medical institutions and the huge general hospital, this part of the city is dotted with sites of interest, such as the Votivkirche, the intimate Freud Museum and the imposing Liechtenstein Museum. The Freyung, a major shopping street, holds bustling street markets.

SIGHTS AT A GLANCE

Streets and Squares
Freyung and Freyung
Passage **1**

Churches and Cathedrals
Votivkirche **4**

Museums and Galleries
Freud Museum **2**
Liechtenstein Museum **3**

SEE ALSO

• *Street Life p37*

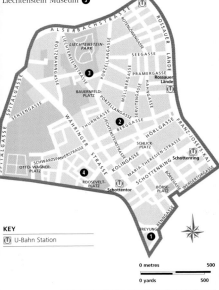

KEY

🚇 U-Bahn Station

| 0 metres | 500 |
| 0 yards | 500 |

◀ *The impressive façade of the 19th-century Votivkirche*

Freyung and Freyung Passage ❶

Map D4.

The Freyung square is surrounded by fine buildings, including the Schottenkirche (1177), its former priory (1155), and the Italian-style Palais Ferstel, dating from 1860. The glass-roofed Freyung Passage, linking Freyung and Herrengasse, is lined with elegant shops. In a small courtyard stands a many-tiered fountain with a lissom Danube water-sprite.

Danube Mermaid's Fountain (1861) in Freyung Passage

Freud Museum ❷

Map C4. Berggasse 19. Open daily. Adm charge.

One of Vienna's most famous addresses, Sigmund Freud, the father of psychoanalysis, lived here from 1891 until he fled the city in 1938. Freud's family home as well as his practice, the flat preserves an intimate domestic atmosphere. Even his hat and cane are on show, together with 420 items of memorabilia, documenting Freud's life.

Schottenkirche on Freyung

Liechtenstein Museum ❸

Map B3. Fürstengasse 1. Open Fri–Mon. Adm charge.

Designed by Domenico Martinelli and completed in 1692, the Liechtenstein Palace was the summer home of the Liechtenstein family and now houses the family's private collection of Baroque art, right through to the 19th century. Behind the imposing Palladian exterior, notable features include the Neo-Classical library, the Hercules Hall and grand staircase with magnificent frescoes. The collection includes masterpieces by many famous artists, such as Raphael, the Brueghels, Van Dyck and Rembrandt, with a special focus on Rubens. The large garden, originally Baroque then English in style, has been recreated and is also open to the public.

A fresco in Palais Liechtenstein

Votivkirche ❹

Map C3. Rooseveltplatz 8. Open Tue–Sun. Free.

After a Hungarian tailor tried - but failed - to assassinate Emperor Franz Joseph on 18 February 1853, his brother, Maximilian, raised funds in gratitude to pay for a new church to be built opposite the Mölker-Bastei, where the attempt had been made. The architect was Heinrich von

Detail on the Votivkirche façade

Ferstel, who began in 1856. The impressive sandstone church, with lacy steeples and spire, was not dedicated until 1879. Many of the Neo-Gothic church's chapels are devoted to Austrian military heroes. The finest monument is the Renaissance sarcophagus tomb of Niklas Salm in a chapel west of the north transept. Salm commanded Austria's forces during the Turkish siege in 1529.

STREET LIFE

RESTAURANTS

Roth
Map C3. Währinger Strasse 1. Tel 01 402 7995.
Cheap
Restaurant with red seating and red panelling on the walls, offering a great selection of Austrian dishes and wines.

Servitenstüberl
Map B4. Servitengasse 7. Tel 01 317 5336. **Medium**
A friendly family-run business, serving Viennese specialities. In summer, it has pleasant outdoor seating overlooking the Servitenkirche.

COFFEE HOUSES

Café Central
Map D4. Herrengasse 14. Vienna's most famous café, situated in the historic Palais Ferstel, has been beautifully restored to its original

splendour. In the late 19th and early 20th centuries, the Central was a renowned meeting place for writers, artists and free thinkers.

Café Berg
Map C4. Berggasse 8.
A trendy hangout with cosy rattan seating and adjoining bookshop. Popular with Vienna's gay community.

SHOPPING

Alt Wiener Christkindlmarkt
Map D4. Freyung.
A real Viennese experience, this bustling market sells all sorts of hand-made objects, baking goodies, candles, gifts, tree decorations, and alcoholic punch and snacks. It is especially magical at night.

See p80 for price codes.

MUSEUM AND TOWNHALL QUARTER

This area has pretty lanes in Josefstadt and many important institutional buildings along the Ringstrasse, as well as superb cultural facilities: the grand Burgtheater and MuseumsQuartier, the Natural History and the Art History Museums.

SIGHTS AT A GLANCE

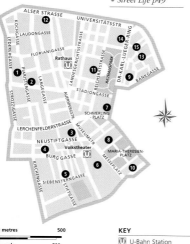

KEY	
Ⓤ	U-Bahn Station

0 metres   500
0 yards   500

◄ The floodlit façade of the Neues Rathaus by night

The 18th-century Maria Treu Kirche, flanked by monastic buildings

Maria Treu Kirche

Map D2. Jodok-Fink-Platz. Open for services and by appointment. Free.

The Piarist church of Maria Treu, founded in 1698, was designed by Johann Lukas von Hildebrandt in 1716 and altered by Matthias Gerl in the 1750s. The elegant twin towers were not completed until 1854. Inside, there is a splendid Baroque frescoed ceiling in vibrant colours, from 1752–3, by the great Austrian painter Franz Anton Maulbertsch. A chapel to the left of the choir contains an altarpiece of the Crucifixion, dating from about 1774, also by Maulbertsch. In front of the church stands a Baroque pillar topped with a statue of the Madonna, attended by statues of saints and angels.

Josefstadt Theatre ❷

Map D2. Josefstädter Strasse 26. Open by appointment only.

This intimate theatre, one of the oldest still standing in Vienna, has enjoyed a great history. Founded in 1788, it was rebuilt by Joseph Kornhäusel in 1822. It has been in operation ever since, accommodating ballet, opera and theatre performances. Beethoven composed and conducted his overture, *The Consecration of the House*, for the 1822 reopening of the theatre after its renovation. Richard Wagner's *Tannhäuser* premiered here in 1857. The director Max Reinhardt supervised the restoration of this attractive theatre in 1924. Today, it puts on mostly light plays and comedies.

Trautson Palace ❸

Map E5. Museumstrasse 7. Closed to the public.

This elegant Baroque palace, designed by Johann Bernhard Fischer von Erlach, was built for Count Trautson in 1710–17. Maria Theresa converted it into guards' headquarters in 1760; today it houses the Justice Ministry. Its central bays jut out with real panache, and above the cornice and pediment stands a large collection of statuary.

St. Ulrichsplatz ❹

Map E2.

This tiny sloping square boasts handsome patrician houses. There is the Schulhaus (mid-1700s) at No. 2, a dainty Baroque house at No. 27 and - next to it - a Renaissance house, which partly obscures the Baroque Ulrichskirche (1721–4). Here the composer Gluck was married in 1750, and Johann Strauss the Younger was christened in 1825.

Spittelberg Pedestrian Area ❺

Map F3.

A group of streets – the pedestrianized Spittelberggasse, Gutenberggasse and Schrankgasse – has been well restored to present a pretty group of 18th- and 19th-century houses. Traditionally the area was lower class and home to the actors, artists and strolling players of the day. The houses were mostly tenements, without gardens or courtyards. The city authorities set about restoring the charming area – with great success. Today restaurants, cafés and boutiques keep the cobbled streets buzzing into the early hours. An arts and crafts market is held every Saturday, from April to November, as well as for Christmas and Easter. The Amerlinghaus theatre, at No. 8 Stiftgasse, is the area's cultural centre and provides a pleasant venue for exhibitions and events.

The façade of the glorious Josefstadt Theatre

The majestic façade of the vast MuseumsQuartier complex

MuseumsQuartier Wien ⑥

Map F3. Museumsplatz 1. Open daily. Guided tours in English by arrangement. Adm charge.

Over 20 different cultural institutions are gathered together in the Museums-Quartier Wien, together with a wide variety of restaurants, cafés and shops. Blending the Baroque architecture of the imperial stables with bold modern buildings, such as the dark grey basalt of the Museum of Modern Art, this impressive complex aims to provide a unique experience.

Museum of Modern Art (MUMOK)

Open Tue–Sun.
The museum contains one of the largest European collections of modern and contemporary art, ranging from American Pop Art, Photo Realism, Fluxus and New Realism to Viennese Actionism, Conceptual and Minimal Art and others from Central and Eastern Europe. The galleries are arranged historically and chrono-logically over five levels.

Architectural Centre Vienna

This centre showcases the diversity of 20th-century building practice in Austria.

Leopold Museum

Open daily.
A white limestone cube hosts a superb collection of Austrian art. Compiled over five decades and displayed on five floors, it counts amongst its treasures works by Klimt and Kokoschka as well as the world's largest Egon Schiele collection.

ZOOM Children's Museum

Book by phone 01 524 7908.
The lively exploration of the world through play is the theme of this innovative centre. The Lab and the Studio Printworks address older children up to 12 years, while a dip in the Ocean is aimed at babies with their parents.

KUNSTHALLE wien

Open daily.
Cross-genre international art, including video and new media, are the focus in this striking red-brick building.

Parliament ❼

Map E3. Dr-Karl-Renner-Ring 3. Open for guided tours Mon–Fri except when in session.

Construction of the immense Neo-Classical building, to plans by Theophil Hansen, began in 1874 and finished in 1884. The raised entrance is approached up a broad ramp. At its foot are the bronze *Horse Tamers* (1901) by sculptor Josef Lax; the ramp itself is decorated with marble figures of Greek and Roman historians. On the roof chariots and impressive statues of ancient scholars and statesmen are displayed. About half the building was destroyed during World War II, and reconstruction was not completed until 1956.

Natural History Museum ❽

Map E3. Maria-Theresia-Platz. Open Wed–Mon. Adm charge.

The Art and Natural History Museums were designed as mirror images by the same architects. The Natural

The Parliament building, with Athena fountain (1902)

History Museum (1889) holds wide-ranging archaeological, anthropological, mineralogical, zoological and geological displays. There are casts of dinosaur skeletons, the world's largest display of skulls illustrating the history of man, gems, Bronze Age items, and extinct birds and mammals. Among its star exhibits is the *Venus of Willendorf*, a 24,000-year-old fertility figure from Lower Austria.

Burgtheater ❾

See pp44–45.

Maria-Theresia-Platz with the Natural History Museum

The Burgtheater **9**

The Burgtheater is one of the most prestigious stages in the German-speaking world. First built during Maria Theresa's reign, the present Italian Renaissance-style building, by Karl von Hasenauer and Gottfried Semper, dates back to 1888.

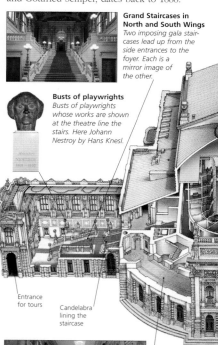

Grand Staircases in North and South Wings
Two imposing gala staircases lead up from the side entrances to the foyer. Each is a mirror image of the other.

Busts of playwrights
Busts of playwrights whose works are shown at the theatre line the stairs. Here Johann Nestroy by Hans Knesl.

Entrance for tours

Candelabra lining the staircase

Foyer
The elegant 60-m (200-ft) long curving foyer serves as a waiting area during intervals. Portraits of famous actors and actresses line its walls.

Auditorium
The central part of the Burgtheater was rebuilt in 1952–5 after war damage, but the auditorium is still decorated in the imperial colours. Here, a critical audience appraises classic and modern plays.

Der Thespiskarren
This ceiling fresco (1886–8) by Gustav Klimt, part of the series The History of the Theatre, depicts Thespis, the first performer of a Greek Tragedy.

Sculpted cherubs on the balustrade (1880–83)

Front Façade
A statue of Apollo (c.1883) presides over a Bacchus frieze by Rudolf Weyr.

VISITORS' CHECKLIST

Map D4. Dr-Karl-Lueger-Ring. Tel (01) 51 444 4440. Open for performances except 24 Dec & Good Fri, Jul & Aug (except guided tours). Guided tours available. Adm charge.
www.burgtheater.at

Museum of Art History façade

Kunsthistorisches Museum ⓾

Map F4. Maria-Theresien-Platz. Open Tue–Sun. Adm charge.

The magnificent building of the Museum of Art History mirrors in style the Museum of Natural History opposite. Built in Italian Renaissance style, by architects Karl von Hasenauer and Gottfried Semper in 1891, it housed for the first time under one roof the artistic treasures assembled over the centuries by the Habsburgs rulers, who were enthusiastic patrons of the arts. Its collection of Old Masters is among the most important in the world.

Italian Collection

Italian paintings from the 15th to 18th centuries, mainly from the Venetian Renaissance, are represented here, including works by Canaletto, Veronese and Titian. Also on show are Tintoretto's *Susanna and the Elders* and Caravaggio's *Madonna and the Rosary*.

Dutch and Flemish Collection

The Dutch section has works by Rembrandt plus a single Vermeer, the enigmatic *The Artists's Studio*. The Flemish section holds about a third of all surviving paintings by Pieter Bruegel the Elder, including the *Peasant Wedding*. Three rooms are devoted to Rubens. They include *The Fur*, an intimate portrait of his wife. Van Dyck is also represented.

Canaletto's painting, View of Vienna from Belvedere *(1759–61)*

Hunters in the Snow (1565) by Pieter Bruegel the Elder

German Collection

Gems in this department are the 16th-century paintings, including several Albrecht Dürer works plus works by Lucas Cranach the Elder and Hans Holbein the Younger.

Spanish Collection

Thanks to Habsburg family ties, Diego Velázques's well-known portraits of the Infanta Margarite Teresa, Philip IV's daughter, made their way into the collection.

Egyptian Antiquities

Four rooms, adorned with Egyptian friezes and motifs, provide the setting for items collected after Napoleon's expedition and excavations at Giza. There is a bust of King Thutmosis III, portraits of Egyptian deities, scarabs, sarcophagi, mummy cases and papyrus books. Among the treasures are the so-called Reserve Head, from the 26th century BC, and a small blue hippopotamus, from a Middle Kingdom royal tomb. Large columns from Aswan are also on display.

Other Collections

Among the museum's other collections are the Greek and Roman Antiquities. One room is laid out like a Roman villa, with marble statues and mosaics. The collection of sculptures and decorative objects includes novelties and intricate automata. Some of the royal patrons worked in the studio themselves; on display is glass blown by Archduke Ferdinand II and Maria Theresa's embroidery. There is also an outstanding cabinet of coins and medals.

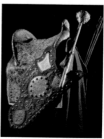

Turkish saddle, mace and quiver from the siege of Vienna in 1683

Neues Rathaus ⑪

Map D3. Friedrich-Schmidt-Platz 1. Guided tours Mon, Wed & Fri and when booked. Free.

The Neo-Gothic town hall - with its spires, stone rosettes, arch windows and loggias - was built by Friedrich von Schmidt in 1883 to express the inhabitants' pride in their city. A huge central tower is topped by the statue of a knight in armour, known as the Rathausmann. The façade has an attractive loggia with delicate tracery and curved balconies. There are seven courtyards; one of these, the Arkadenhof, hosts summer concerts. All year round various festivals take place on the square in front of the Rathaus, ranging from a large Christmas market to a summer music film festival. The grand building looks spectacular when floodlit.

16th-century crucifix by Veit Stoss, in the Dreifaltigkeitskirche

Dreifaltigkeitskirche ⑫

Map C2. Alser Strasse 17. Open daily. Free.

The church of the Holy Trinity (1685–1727) contains an altarpiece (1708) in the north aisle, by Martino Altomonte, and a crucifix in the south aisle, from Veit Stoss' workshop. Beethoven's body was brought here after he died in 1827. Following the funeral service, which was attended by Schubert and the poet Franz Grillparzer, his coffin was taken to the cemetery at Währing.

Dreimäderlhaus ⑬

Map D4. Schreyvogelgasse 10. Closed to the public.

The houses on one side of this cobbled street are a delightful remnant of Biedermeier Vienna. The prettiest is the Dreimäderlhaus (1803). There is a story that Schubert had three sweethearts (drei Mäderl) ensconced here, but it is more likely that the house was named after the 1920s operetta, *Dreimäderlhaus*, which uses his melodies.

Front façade of the Neues Rathaus, with its 98-m- (320-ft-) high tower

University 🄸

Map D3–4. Dr-Karl-Lueger-Ring 1. Open Mon–Sat. Free.

Founded in 1365 by Duke Rudolf IV, the university's present home dates from 1883. In 1895 Gustav Klimt was commissioned to decorate the hall with frescoes, but the authorities objected to the nudity on show. The frescoes were destroyed in World War II. The courtyard is lined with busts of distinguished professors, including the philosopher Franz Brentano and Sigmund Freud.

One of the arcades surrounding the University courtyard

Pasqualati Haus 🄸

Map D4. Mölker-Bastei 8. Open Tue–Sun. Adm charge.

The Pasqualati Haus is the most famous of Beethoven's many homes in Vienna. In 1804–08 and 1810–15, he lived and composed many of his best-loved works here, including the Symphonies Nos. 4, 5, 7 and 8, *Fidelio*, Piano Concerto No. 4 and string quartets. The rooms he occupied on the fourth floor now display various memorabilia, such as a lock of his hair and early editions of his scores.

STREET LIFE

RESTAURANTS

Spatzennest
Map E2. St-Ulrichsplatz 1. Tel 01 526 1659. **Cheap**
Delightful place close to the Spittelberg pedestrian area. Appetising Viennese dishes; excellent value.

Wiener Rathauskeller
Map D3. Rathausplatz 1. Tel 01 405 1210. **Medium**
Restaurant and wine tavern under the town hall, serving top Austrian fare in vaulted surroundings, often to the sounds of folk or waltzes.

COFFEE HOUSES

Café Landtmann
Map D4. Dr-Karl-Lueger-Ring 4.
Regulars at this Vienna landmark have included Sigmund Freud, Gustav Mahler, Max Reinhardt, Marlene Dietrich and Paul McCartney. Always crowded. Extensive menu, homemade desserts and pastries, but quite expensive.

SHOPPING

Vinoe
Map E2. Piaristengasse 35.
Top wines from Lower Austria are on sale here at reasonable prices. Plus other regional products (juices, brandies, oils, jams, chocolate).

Cadê? natur.textil.design.
Map E2. Strozzigasse 2
One of Vienna's top fashion labels, specializing in natural fabrics, designed, made and sold in this shop.

See p80 for price codes

OPERA AND NASCHMARKT

An area of huge contrasts, including the stately Opera House as well as trendy Mariahilfer Strasse. The other major thoroughfare in this area is Linke Wienzeile, which runs parallel to Rechte Wienzeile, both following the bends of the river Wien. Between these roads is the bustling Naschmarkt, which is overlooked by Otto Wagner's superbly elegant Art Nouveau apartments.

SIGHTS AT A GLANCE

Streets and Squares
Mariahilfer Strasse **6**

Historic Buildings
Hotel Sacher **2**
Opera House pp52–3 **1**

Secession Building **3**
Wagner Apartments **5**

Markets
Naschmarkt **4**

SEE ALSO

● *Street Life p55*

KEY

Ⓤ U-Bahn Station

◀ *Main staircase and hallway at the Opera House*

The Opera House ❶

Vienna's Neo-Renaissance Staatsoper opened in 1869 with Mozart's *Don Giovanni*. After bomb damage in 1945, it received a new auditorium and high-tech stage. The Opera House reopened on 5 November 1955 with a performance of Beethoven's *Fidelio*.

Gustav Mahler by Rodin

Grand Staircase
A grand marble staircase, with statues of the seven liberal arts by Josef Gasser, sweeps up from the main entrance.

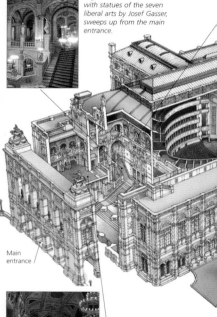

Main entrance

Schwind Foyer
16 oil paintings by Moritz von Schwind hang in this foyer. They depict famous operas, including Fidelio and The Barber of Seville.

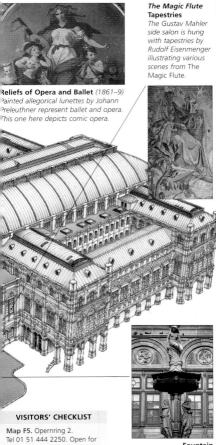

The Magic Flute Tapestries
The Gustav Mahler side salon is hung with tapestries by Rudolf Eisenmenger illustrating various scenes from The Magic Flute.

Reliefs of Opera and Ballet *(1861–9)*
Painted allegorical lunettes by Johann Preleuthner represent ballet and opera. This one here depicts comic opera.

Fountain
On either side of the Opera House stand two graceful fountains, designed by Hans Gasser.

VISITORS' CHECKLIST

Map F5. Opernring 2.
Tel 01 51 444 2250. Open for performances. Open daily for guided tours. State Opera Museum. Goethegasse 1. Open Tue–Sun. Adm charge.
www.wiener-staatsoper.at

Relief on the façade of the Secession Building

Opera House ❶

See pp52–3.

Hotel Sacher ❷

Map F4. Philharmonikerstrasse 4. Open daily.

The hotel was founded in 1876 by the son of Franz Sacher, who, according to some, was the creator of the famous Sachertorte in 1840. In 1892–1930, under the management of Anna Sacher, the founder's cigar-smoking daughter-in-law, it became a venue for the extra-marital affairs of the rich and noble, counting emperors, diplomats and artists among its guests. Having become a Viennese institution, the Hotel Sacher is today still a discreetly sumptuous hotel, ranking among the city's finest.

Naschmarkt

Secession Building ❸

Map F4. Friedrichstrasse 12. Open Tue–Sun. Adm charge.

This unusual Art Nouveau building was designed by Joseph Maria Olbrich as a showcase for the Secession movement's artists. The almost windowless building is a squat cube with four towers, topped with a filigree globe of entwined laurel leaves. The motto of the founders, emblazoned in gold on the façade, translates as, "To every Age its Art, to Art its Freedom". Gustav Klimt's *Beethoven Frieze* is the best-known exhibit. The painting, designed in 1902 and thought to be a commentary on Beethoven's Ninth Symphony, has groups of figures on three walls.

Naschmarkt ❹

Map G4.

Vienna's liveliest market has many well-established shops and some of the best snack bars in Vienna. At its western end are florists', wine producers' and farmers' stalls and a Saturday flea market. At No. 6 Kettenbrückengasse is the simple flat where Franz Schubert died in 1828. On display are prints, facsimiles and a family piano.

Wagner Apartments 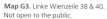 ❺

Map G3. Linke Wienzeile 38 & 40.
Not open to the public.

Otto Wagner designed these superb apartment buildings, overlooking the Naschmarkt, in 1899. They represent the apex of Art Nouveau. No. 40, the more striking of the two, is known as Majolikahaus after the glazed pottery used for the façade. It is subtly decorated with flower motifs in pink, blue and green. Even the sills are moulded and decorated. No. 38 has sparkling gilt ornament, mostly by Kolo Moser.

Mariahilfer Strasse ❻

Map G1, G2, F3.

After Kärnter Strasse and the Graben, this street is Vienna's trendiest and busiest shopping mile. It is lined with numerous shops and department stores, restaurants, cafés, ice-cream parlours and cinemas. The shops are joined by two churches: Stiftskirche (1739), at the lower end, has an austere pyramidal façade rising to a bulbous steeple. Mariahilf, in the middle of the street, is Baroque in style and dominated by two towers.

The Majolikahaus, one of the Art Nouveau Wagner Apartments

STREET LIFE

RESTAURANTS

Hungerkünstler
Map G3. Gumpendorfer Strasse 48. Tel 01 587 9210.
Medium
Reliably good Viennese and international cuisine.

Mango
Map F3. Theobaldgasse 11. Tel 01 587 4758. **Expensive**
Latin America-influenced

restaurant, using mango as an ingredient in all its dishes.

CAFÉ

Naschmarkt Deli
Map G4. Naschmarkt stall 421–36.
Serves excellent breakfasts all day long and ethnic food, from Viennese to Turkish.

See p80 for price codes.

BELVEDERE QUARTER

This extravagant district houses the Baroque Karlskirche and two huge palaces: the Belvedere and the Schwarzenberg Palace. North of the church are the Musikverein, home to the Vienna Philharmonic, the Wien Museum Karlsplatz and the stylish Karlsplatz Pavilions. Further south, the Undertakers' Museum charts the Viennese fascination with death.

SIGHTS AT A GLANCE

Historic Buildings
Karlsplatz Pavilions **4**
Musikverein **3**
Schwarzenbergplatz **5**
Theresianum **9**

Museums and Galleries
Bestattungsmuseum **8**
Wien Museum Karlsplatz **2**

Palaces and Gardens
  of the Belvedere **6**

Parks and Gardens
Botanical Gardens **7**

Churches
Karlskirche **1**

SEE ALSO

• *Street Life p61*

KEY

U   U-Bahn Station

🚋   Badner Bahn stop

| 0 metres | | 500 |
| 0 yards | | 500 |

◀ *Botanical Gardens*

Karlskirche ❶

Map G5. Karlsplatz. Open daily. Adm charge.

During Vienna's plague epidemic in 1713, Emperor Karl VI vowed that as soon as the city was delivered from its plight he would build a church dedicated to St Charles Borromeo (1538–84), patron saint of plague victims. Johann Bernhard Fischer von Erlach designed the richly eclectic Baroque masterpiece, built in 1715–37. The gigantic dome and portico are borrowed from classical architecture, while there are Oriental echoes in the gatehouses and minaret-like columns. The pediment has a statue of the saint by Govanni Stanetti and reliefs showing the suffering of the Viennese, 8,000 of whom died from the plague. The interior is richly embellished with carvings and altarpieces by the foremost artists of the day, including paintings by Daniel Gran and Martino Altomonte. Two *putti* surmount the gilded pulpit, decorated with *rocailles* and flower garlands.

The pulpit in Karlskirche

Wien Museum Karlsplatz ❷

Map G5. Karlsplatz. Open Tue–Sun. Adm charge.

Unremarkable on the outside, this museum does hold a few gems worth seeing. Over three storeys it documents 7,000 years of the city's history as well as the lives of prominent Viennese (such as Gustav Klimt, Egon Schiele, Franz Grillparzer). There are the original plans for Schönbrunn Palace, silver- and glassware by Josef Hoffmann and designs from the Wiener Werkstätte.

Façade of the Musikverein

Musikverein ❸

Map F5. Börsendorferstrasse 12. Open for concerts only. Ticket charge.

The Musikverein building, built to designs by Theophil Hansen in 1867–9, is the home of the Society of the Friends of Music whose aim is to promote music in all its facets. It became world famous when the Vienna Philharmonic Orchestra began giving their annual New Year's concert here in 1941. There are three concert halls. The Golden Hall, which seats almost 2,000, is the finest, with lavish decorations in blue and gold and excellent acoustics.

Sunflower motifs on the façade of the Karlsplatz Pavilions

Karlsplatz Pavilions ❹

Map F5. Karlsplatz. Open Tue–Sun in summer. Free.

In the late 19th century, Otto Wagner designed and engineered many aspects of the Vienna City Train, the horse-drawn, then steam-powered predecessors of today's underground system. In total Wagner designed 34 stations, but none can match this stylish steel and marble pair (1898–9) on Karlsplatz, also known as Wagner Pavilions. Gilt sunflowers are stamped onto the marble cladding and eaves. But the greatest impact is achieved by the curving green copper roofs. One pavilion is now a café, the other once facing it is an exhibition space.

Schwarzenbergplatz ❺

Map G5–6.

At the centre of this square is the equestrian statue (1867) of Prince Schwarzenberg who led the Austrian army against Napoleon at the Battle of Leipzig (1813). The square combines huge office blocks, the busy Ringstrasse and the Baroque splendour of the Schwarzenberg and Belvedere palaces. Behind Hochstrahlbrunnen fountain (1873) is the Liberation monument (1945), a vivid reminder of the city's post-war history, when it was occupied by the four Allied Powers. Schwarzenberg-platz, in the Soviet zone, was then renamed Stalinplatz.

The enormous Hochstrahlbrunnen in Schwarzenbergplatz

Steps in the middle area of the garden, featuring putti (1852)

Palaces and Gardens of the Belvedere ❻

Map G6, H6. Upper Belvedere: Prinz-Eugen-Strasse 27. Lower Belvedere: Rennweg 6a. Open Tue–Sun, except after Easter & Whit Mon, 24 & 25 Dec. Adm charge.

The Belvedere was built by Johann Lukas von Hildebrandt as the summer residence of Prince Eugene of Savoy, the military commander whose strategies helped vanquish the Turks in 1683. Situated on a gently sloping hill, the complex consists of two palaces linked by a formal garden laid out in the French style by Dominique Girard. The garden is sited on three levels, conveying a complicated system of classical allusions.

Statues of sphinxes

The Upper Belvedere

The Upper Belvedere has an elaborate façade and sweeping entrance. Baroque stairways lead to the ceremonial rooms and the Marble Hall, used for state occasions. Today, the building houses 19th- and 20th-century paintings, including works by Caspar David Friedrich, Egon Schiele and Oskar Kokoschka. Also held here is Klimt's most famous work, *The Kiss* (1909).

The Lower Belvedere

Prince Eugene's everyday quarters now hold the Museum of Austrian Baroque, with works from Vienna's Golden Age (1683–1780). Among the artists shown are Daniel Gran, Georg Raphael Donner and Martino Altomonte. The Orangery next door houses medieval art and sculptures.

The majestic façade of the Upper Belvedere

The Botanical Gardens

Botanical Gardens ❼

Map G7. Rennweg 14. Open daily Easter–mid-Oct and in winter (weather permitting). Free.

The Botanical Gardens were created in 1754 by Maria Theresa and her physician, van Swieten, for cultivating medicinal herbs. Expanded to their present shape in the 19th century, they remain a centre for the study of plant sciences as part of the University of Vienna's Institute of Botany. The gardens now contain over 9,000 plant species, arranged geographically. There is a temperate greenhouse, living fossils, an alpine garden and carnivorous plants. The gardens offer a quiet spot to sit and relax after sightseeing.

Bestattungsmuseum ❽

Map J6. Goldeggasse 19. Open Mon–Fri (guided tours by appointment only).

The undertakers' museum, opened in 1967, provides a unique overview of death cults and funeral rites. Over 1,000 funeral objects are on show here, including a stiletto the doctors used to ensure a patient was really dead, re-usable coffins with a trapdoor and ways to dress up a corpse seated on a chair for one last photograph.

Theresianum ❾

Map H5. Favoritenstrasse 15. Closed to the public.

A favourite summer residence of several emperors, Maria Theresa handed the Baroque building over to the Jesuits in 1746. The latter established a college here for the education of lesser aristocrats. Today, it is still a school and, since 1964, it has also been a college for diplomats and civil servants.

STREET LIFE

RESTAURANTS

Maestro
Map F5. Lothringerstrasse 20/ Heumarkt 6. Tel 01 242 00 740.
Expensive
Sophisticated Viennese cuisine in the magnificent Konzerthaus. Great for a luxury meal.

CAFES AND BARS

Salm Bräu
Map G6. Rennweg 8.
Cheap
Beer-cellar serving hearty local food, including sausages, and home-brewed beer.

Café Schwarzenberg
Map F5. Kärntner Ring 17.
Traditional Viennese café with opulent velvet seating and mirrors on the walls. Hosts changing exhibitions and piano concerts.

SHOPPING

Swarovski
Map F5. Kärntner Strasse 8.
All things crystal and shiny are on sale here, from gifts to jewellery and collectibles.

See p80 for price codes.

FURTHER AFIELD

Some of Vienna's most interesting sights are outside the city centre. At Schönbrunn sprawls Maria Theresa's vast palace, while the Klosterneuburg monastery houses great ecclesiastical art treasures. The Prater, Augarten and Lainzer Tiergarten offer great recreational spaces.

SIGHTS AT A GLANCE

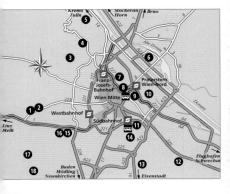

KEY

 Main line railway station

🚌 Coach and bus station

0 km   4

0 miles   4

◀ *Part of the façade of the Hundertwasser Haus, built in 1985*

Detail of the Brunnenhaus (1913)

Wagner Villas ❶

Hüttelbergstrasse 26, Penzing.
Open Mon–Fri. Adm charge.

This grand Art Nouveau villa, incorporating Ionic columns, was built by Otto Wagner in 1886–8. The present owner, the painter Ernst Fuchs, has added his own statues and garish colours. The steel-and-concrete Brunnenhaus next door is decorated in a severe geometrical style, with deep blue panels and nailhead decoration. The glass ornament is by Kolo Moser.

Kirche am Steinhof ❷

Baumgartner Höhe 1, Penzing.
Phone for opening times.
Adm charge.

Otto Wagner's last work, the church (1907) exterior is marble-clad with nailhead ornament, spindly pillars and columns with angels and saints. The interior is a single space with shallow side chapels. Gold and white friezes and roof panels, with gilt nailhead ornamentation, are lit through blue glass windows by Kolo Moser.

Geymüller Schlössl ❸

Khevenhüllerstrasse 2, Währing.
To view make phone appointment. Adm charge.

The little palace (1808), built for the banker Johann Heinrich von Geymüller, is now a branch of the Museum of Applied Arts. Its collection comprises Biedermeier and Empire furniture and items such as spittoons, painted porcelain and 200 clocks dating from 1780 to 1850.

Courtyard at the Passauer Hof, an old wine press house

Grinzing ❹

Once a small vintners' village on the outskirts of the city, Grinzing is today the hub of the *Heurigen*, with crowds of both locals and tourists flocking to the wine taverns. The most authentic are to be found in Sandgasse and the lower town. Repeatedly destroyed by Turkish troops during the sieges, and again by Napoleon in 1809, the village is nonetheless pretty.

Art Nouveau angels decorating the façade of Kirche am Steinhof

The Baroque façade of the Augarten Palace

Klosterneuburg ❺

Stift Klosterneuburg. Open daily.
Guided tours. Adm charge.

In the ancient town of
Klosterneuburg, 13 km
(8 miles) north of Vienna,
stands the vast monastery of
the same name. Founded in
the early 12th century by the
Babenberg ruler Leopold III,
it houses the astonishing
Verduner Altar, completed in
1181. In the 18th century the
abbey was expanded by Karl
VI, who tried to equal the
scale of the Madrid Escorial
palace. Work was halted
after his death in 1740.

Danube Park ❻

Alte Donau. Open daily. Free.

The Danube Park adjoins
UNO-City, the complex of
United Nations agencies.
Laid out in 1964 on a former
rubbish dump, the park has
cycle paths, cafés and other
amenities. Rising 252 m
(827 ft) above the park is
the Danube Tower, with two
revolving restaurants and
an observation platform.
On clear days, you can see
Bratislava in the Slovak
Republic from the tower.

Augarten Palace and Park ❼

Obere Augartenstrasse 1.
Palace closed to the public.
Park open daily. Porcelain
Museum open Mon–Sat.

An earlier palace on this site
was destroyed by the Turks
in 1683 and then rebuilt
(c.1700) to a design attributed
to Johann Bernhard Fischer
von Erlach. Since 1948 it has
been the home of the famous
Vienna Boys' Choir.

The Augarten has the
oldest Baroque garden in
Vienna, with topiary lining
long paths shaded by walls
of foliage. Planted in the 17th
century, it was opened to
the public in 1775 by Joseph
II. Mozart, Beethoven and
Johann Strauss I all gave
concerts in the park.

The Augarten was also
used for royal receptions
and meetings during the
Congress of Vienna in 1815.
The pavilion used to be the
imperial porcelain factory,
founded in the 18th century,
but has been run since the
1920s by the municipal
authorities. Its showroom
has displays on the history
of Augarten porcelain.

Hundertwasser Haus

Kriminalmuseum **8**

Grosse Sperlgasse 24. Open Thu–Sun.

Located in a medieval house is this fascinating museum of crime. In 20 rooms, it offers a blend of documentary social history and a chamber of horrors, which portrays the darker side of Viennese life from the Middle Ages till today. There is a wide selection of murder weapons, the mummified heads of executed criminals, death masks and case histories illustrated with photographs and prints. Political crime, such as the lynching of a government minister during the 1848 revolution, is also covered.

Painting depicting a 1782 robbery

Hundertwasser Haus **9**

Löwengasse/Kegelgasse. Closed to the public.

The Hundertwasser Haus is a municipal apartment block, designed in 1985 by the flamboyant Austrian artist Friedensreich Hundertwasser as a playful take on usually dull social housing. The building's façade sports irregular bands of colour, spires with onion dome cupolas and trees on the rooftop. All the windows vary in size and shape, each one is framed by a complementary colour. The size of each of the 50 apartments is visibly marked by an uneven line of ceramic tiles. Today it houses 200 tenants and has become one of Vienna's most visited landmarks.

A ride at the Prater funfair

Prater **10**

Praterstern. Open daily mid-Mar–end Sep. Ferris Wheel daily except 24 Dec.

Opened to the public in 1766, the Prater is the most popular city park. During the 19th century its western end became a huge funfair catering for the Viennese workers, with beer gardens, booths, sideshows and the Ferris Wheel (1896) of *The Third Man* fame.

Heeresgeschichtliches Museum 11

Arsenal, Ghegastrasse Objekt 18.
Open Sat–Thu except 1 Jan.
Easter Sun, 1 May, 1 Nov, 24, 25
& 31 Dec. Adm charge.

The impressive museum of army history was designed by Theophil Hansen in 1856. Exhibits relate to the Turkish siege of 1683, the French Revolution and the Napoleonic wars. Don't miss the car in which Archduke Franz Ferdinand was assassinated, starting World War I.

Exhibit in the Tank Park

Central Cemetery 12

Simmeringer Hauptstrasse 234.
Open daily. Free.

Europe's largest burial ground, containing two and a half million graves, was opened in 1874 on the city's southern outskirts. Its central section includes graves of artists, composers, architects, writers and local politicians. Among the city's musicians buried here are Johann Strauss I and II, Beethoven, Brahms and Schubert. There is a memorial to Mozart who is buried in St Marx cemetery. Funerals in Vienna are quite lavish affairs, as the Viennese like to be buried in style, appropriate to their station in life. The cemetery contains funerary statues, varying from the humble to the bombastic, paying tribute to the city's enduring obsession with death.

Favoriten Water Tower

Favoriten Water Tower 13

Windtenstrasse 3, Favoriten.
Open for guided tours (phone
01 599 593 1006 to arrange).

The Favoriten pumping station was constructed in 1889 to supply the rapidly growing city with drinking water. Only the 67-m (220-ft) high yellow-and-red-brick water tower and its original pumping equipment remain, standing in a stark contrast to the ornate turrets, pinnacles and tiles of the building's superstructure. The interior has recently been restored.

Grave of Johann Strauss I and II

Façade of Schönbrunn Palace seen from the gardens

Amalienbad

Reumannplatz 23, Favoriten.
Open Tue–Sat. Adm charge.

The Art Nouveau Amalien-
bad (1923–6) is a perfect
example of a public amenity
combining usefulness with
style. The two designers,
Otto Nadel and Karl Schmal-
hofer, were employees of
the city's architectural department. The magnificent main
pool is covered by a glass
roof that can be opened and
is surrounded by galleries
overlooking the pool. Elsewhere in the building are
saunas and smaller baths
and pools used for therapeu-
tic purposes. When first
opened, the baths were
one of the largest in Europe,
accommodating about 1,300
people. The interior features
imaginative mosaic and tile
decoration. Damaged in
World War II, the baths were
impeccably restored in 1986.

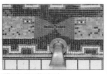

Tiles in Amalienbad

Schönbrunn Palace and Gardens

Schönbrunner Schlossstrasse 47.
Palace and Gardens open daily.
Adm charge.

The former summer resi-
dence of the imperial family
takes its name from a spring
on this site. Leopold I asked
Johann Bernhard Fischer
von Erlach to design a grand
Baroque residence here in
1695. It was completed in
the mid-18th century by
Nikolaus Pacassi for Maria
Theresa. The strict symmetry
of the architecture is comple-
mented by the gardens, with
fountains and statues framed
by trees and alleyways.

The Maze in Schönbrunn Gardens

Inside the Palace

The interior was designed in
stunning Rococo style for
Marias Theresa. White-and-
gold stucco, tall windows,
splendid chandeliers, crystal
mirrors, Flemish tapestries,

The pavilion at Schönbrunn Zoo

wood panelling and superb frescoes feature large. The Grand Gallery is particularly spectacular. But don't miss the Mirror and Porcelain Rooms, or the Chinese-style Blue Salon and Vieux-Laque Room.

The Gardens

The formal French Baroque park was laid out as a large pleasure garden by Nicolaus Jadot and Adrian von Steckhoven during the reign of Maria Theresa. In the park stand the world's second largest Baroque Orangery, the impressive steel-and-glass Palm House built in 1881–2 by Segenschmid, Roman ruin follies and countless mythical statues. There is also a coach museum and the world's oldest zoo, home to some 750 animals.

Kaiser Pavilion **16**

Schönbrunner Schlossstrasse 13, Hietzing. Open Tue–Sun Apr–Oct. Free.

Otto Wagner built this railway station – a white cube with green iron-work, a copper dome and a cupola with glass-and-gilt flower decoration – for the imperial family in 1899 to showcase his work. The panelled waiting room has an asymmetrical carpet, and a stylish marble and brass fireplace.

Lainzer Tiergarten **17**

Lainzer Tiergarten, Hietzing. Open daily mid-Feb–mid-Nov.

A former Habsburg hunting ground, the immense nature reserve in the Vienna Woods was opened to the public in 1923. A 24-km (15-mile) stone wall protects its herds of deer and wild boar. In the grounds stands the Hermes Villa (1884), a retreat for the imperial family. Inside it has murals with scenes from *A Midsummer Night's Dream*, as well as exhibitions.

Wotruba Kirche **18**

Georgsgasse/Rysergasse, Mauer. Open Thu–Sun in summer or by phone appointment. Free.

This church, built in 1974–6 by Fritz Mayer, was based on uncompromisingly modern designs by the sculptor Fritz Wotruba. Raw in style but powerfully compact, its piles of irregular concrete slabs look different from every angle. Huge glass panels illuminate the interior, which accommodates a congregation of up to 250.

The Kaiser Pavilion railway station

DAY TRIPS FROM VIENNA

A short distance from the capital there is an astonishing range of beautiful countryside to explore on day or weekend trips away from the city. To the west lie the verdant Vienna Woods, perfect for long walks or cycle rides. There are idyllic spa towns, such as Baden, to explore and the Mayerling chapel to visit, commemorating a tragic double suicide. On the border to Hungary lies the jewel of Neusiedler See, a vast steppe lake, surrounded by attractive resorts, with swimming, boating and wind-surfing facilities. South of Vienna is Eisenstadt, associated mainly with the Esterházy family and Franz Liszt. Further in the south-west is Mariazell, the main site in Europe for Catholic pilgrimages.

SIGHTS AT A GLANCE

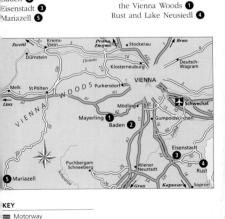

KEY

■ Motorway

■ Major road

■ Minor road

■ Airport

0 km   20

0 miles   20

◁ A wintry scene in the Vienna Woods

Mayerling and the Vienna Woods ❶

Mayerling Chapel. Open daily except 1 Jan, Good Fri, 25 Dec. Ring bell for attention.

The Wienerwald, or Vienna Woods, to the west of the city, is a favourite weekend destination for the Viennese. Crossed by walking and cycling tracks, the wooded hills cover an area of 1,250 sq km (480 sq miles).

One of the most visited sights is the Mayerling hunting lodge, now a chapel. It was the scene in 1889 of the double suicide of Crown Prince Rudolf, heir to the Austro-Hungarian throne, and his 17-year-old mistress, Mary Vetsera. Mary had drunk poison and Rudolf had then shot himself. The reasons for the tragedy remain shrouded in mystery. It shook the entire Austro-Hungarian empire and even became the subject of films and musicals. After his son's death, the distraught Emperor Franz Joseph gave the hunting lodge to a Carmelite convent.

Mary Vetsera's tombstone

Monument to the composer Strauss in the spa park in Baden

Baden ❷

Baden, south of Vienna, has curative sulphurous springs and hot pools of 36°C (97°F) dating back to Roman times. The spa had its heyday in the early 1800s when it was popular with the court, and many of the villas, baths and a large park were built.

Eisenstadt ❸

Schloss. Open daily summer, winter guided tours only. Adm charge. Haydn Museum. Open daily summer, winter by appt. only

In Eisenstadt, southeast of Vienna, is the grand Schloss Esterházy, built for Prince Paul Esterházy in 1663–73. It contains the Haydnsaal, a great hall of state decorated with 18th-century frescoes, where Joseph Haydn conducted. He lived nearby on Haydngasse; his house is now a museum.

ust and
eusiedl Lake ⑥

he Neusiedler See, part of
which is in Hungary, covers
n area of 320 sq km (124 sq
ile). Apart from the Wulka
iver, the lake has no natural
n- or outlets. The water is
ightly saline and not more
han 2 m (6½ ft) deep, so it
warms up early in summer.
he banks are overgrown
with reeds, which make
deal nesting grounds for
irds. The reeds are also
sed locally for thatching
nd basketwork.

Around the lake are beach
esorts, boating harbours
nd wine villages, of which
ust is the prettiest. It has a
erfectly preserved old town
with many Renaissance and
aroque buildings. Star
ghts include the town hall
nd Fischerkirche. It is also
nown for the storks which
est on its roofs and towers.
The lake and surroundings
ave been a UNESCO World
Heritage Site since 2001.

The pretty wine village of Rust

Mariazell ⑤

Basilica open daily. Free.

Mariazell has been Central
Europe's main Catholic
pilgrim site and a Gothic and
Baroque basilica, enlarged
in the 17th century, testifies
to its religious significance.
Inside is a wealth of Baroque
stucco, painting and decoration. The treasury also forms
part of the church. A cable
car up the mountain leaves
every 20 minutes from the
town centre. The world's
oldest steam tram (1884),
runs between Mariazell
station and a nearby lake.

…nitz, one of the resorts on Lake Neusiedl

Getting Around

The Vienna city centre is compact, making most sights accessible on foot. Public transport consists of a tram, bus and underground network. All the services are clean, efficient and easy to use and operate from 5am to 12:30am.

Walking

Walking is an excellent way to see the city, but make sure you stop when the red figure shows or you could be fined on the spot. In addition, keep an eye out for cyclists; they share the pavement with pedestrians. For information on guided walking tours on offer in and around the city, including those conducted in English, contact the Wiener Tourismusverband.

Tram stop symbol

Tram

Travelling on a red-and-white *Strassenbahn* is a great way to see the city – lines 1 and 2 take you to all the main sights round Ringstrasse. Destinations are displayed on the front of the tram; ticket prices are the same as on the *U-Bahn*.

Underground station symbol

Underground

Vienna's Underground or *U-Bahn* system is one of the most modern in Europe. A clean, fast and reliable service, it also takes you further afield. There are currently five colour-coded lines, with line U2 running in a circle around the city. Tickets need to be bought beforehand and validated by insertion into a stamping machine. Train doors are opened manually – give them a sharp tug.

Bus stop symbol

Bus

Small red-and-white hoppe buses serve the city centre, larger buses travel to the suburbs. Night buses leave from Schwedenplatz every day throughout the night at 30-minute intervals.

*Logos for Schnellbahn (left) and
Bundesbahn (right)*

Trains

The *Schnellbahn* (S-Bahn
for short) with a blue-and-
white logo, and the local
Bundesbahn trains are both
commuter services. Visitors
will find the north–south
S-Bahn trunk line and the
S7 to the airport useful.
Both types of train also
allow you to reach sights
that are further afield.

Tram ticket machine

Tickets

Tickets can be purchased
as you board a bus or tram
but it is more convenient
and cheaper to buy a pass
or a strip ticket in advance,
from U- or S-Bahn stations
or from newsagents (*Tabak
Trafik*). Stamp them when
you start your journey. A
standard ticket covers all
parts of Vienna (zone 100).
You can change trains and
modes of transport as many
times as necessary if you
don't break your journey.

Fiaker

To explore the city in a
more leisurely fashion,
a horse-drawn cab, known
as *Fiaker*, is a good way to
get around. Once Vienna's
taxi transport, they are
today used mainly for ceremonial purposes and as a
tourist attraction. *Fiaker*
ranks are outside the opera
house, the Hofburg and
next to Stephansdom.

*Signs: exit, regional train, S-Bahn,
ticket machine, regional bus*

Driving in Vienna

Driving is on the right, and
priority is always to the
right unless otherwise indi-
cated. You must give way
to trams, buses and emer-
gency vehicles. The speed
limit in Vienna is 50 kph
(30 mph), and the limit for
alcohol is 0,5 mg (about
1 glass of wine). Police can
check and spot-fine you.

Parking spaces are scarce.
Don't park between *Anfang*
(start) and *Ende* (end) signs.
You can buy 24-hour parking
disks for Park & Pay areas in
districts 1–9 at newsagents.

A car park sign, signalling spaces

Survival Guide

Many sights are busy at the weekend, so plan your visits during the week if you can. Shops open Monday to Friday 8am to 6pm and until 5pm on Saturdays; banks are closed at the weekend. Vienna is a safe city, and help is quickly at hand.

COMMUNICATIONS

Post Offices

Yellow-fronted post offices are usually open 8am–noon and 2–6pm Mon–Fri. Post offices in railway stations and the main office in Fleischmarkt 19 are open around the clock. You can make phone calls from a post office and pay afterwards. Letter boxes are bright yellow.

Post office sign

MONEY

Currency

The official currency in Austria is the euro, with cents as the smaller units. Banknotes are available in denominations of 5, 10, 20, 50, 100, 200 and 500 euros; coins 1 and 2 euros and 1, 2, 5, 10, 20 and 50 cents.

Yellow letter box

Telephones

Public telephone booths can be found almost everywhere and in some public buildings. Some are card-operated; phonecards can be bought at tobacconists, newsagents or at post offices. The international dialling code for Austria is 0043 and 01 for Vienna. The mobile phone network is well developed and your mobile should work well all over the city, including on the underground, provided it is cleared for roaming.

Autobank automatic money dispensing machine

Cash and Credit

Cash dispensers are easily spotted, mostly next to banks. Look for the blue and green letter "B". Cash is used more widely than credit cards; check before running up a high bill.

HEALTH

Austria has one of the finest health care systems in Europe. No expense is spared, and you can probably expect a service at least as good as that at home.

Insurance

Visitors from EU countries will need a European health insurance card which gives you free or reduced cost treatment. It is available online, by phone or from the post office.

Pharmacies

If you are not in an emergency, a pharmacist can advise you on medicines and treatment. Pharmacies, called *Apotheke*, are identified by a red "A" outside. Outside opening hours, closed pharmacies display the address of the nearest open chemists. You can also find this information in the telephone directory, or by phoning the emergency pharmacy service who have a recorded-message service in German.

Policeman

Pharmacy sign

SAFETY

Unfortunately, crime levels have risen, and muggings are now as common as elsewhere. However, the police are omnipresent in case of trouble.

Police

Emergency numbers can be called for free from public phones. Police stations are located all across Vienna. You should report any crime.

Pickpockets

This is probably the most likely crime you could encounter. As a tourist you are a potential target. Protect your belongings, particularly in queues and in busy places, and while withdrawing cash.

Facade of a pharmacy

EMERGENCY NUMBERS

Police: 133
Ambulance: 144
Fire: 122
Night and weekend
  emergency doctor: 141
  emergency dentist
  (recording): 01 512 20 78
  emergency pharmacy
  (recording): 1550

Index

Acknowledgments

Dorling Kindersley would like to thank the following people whose help and assistance contributed to the preparation of this book.

Design and Editorial

Publisher Douglas Amrine
Publishing Manager Vivien Antwi
Design Managers Sunita Gahir, Mabel Chan
Cartography Casper Morris
Editorial Alex Farrel, Pollyanna Poulter
Production Controller Shane Higgins
Picture Research Ellen Root
DTP Natasha Lu
Jacket Design Tessa Bindloss

Picture Credits

Every effort has been made to trace the copyright holders, and we apologize in advance for any omissions. We would be pleased to insert appropriate acknowledgements in any subsequent edition of this publication.

t = top; tl = top left; tc = top centre; tr = top right; cla = centre left above; ca = centre above; cra = centre right above; cl = centre left; c = centre; cr = centre right; clb = centre left below; cb = centre below; crb = centre right below; bl = bottom left; b = bottom; bc = bottom centre; br = bottom right.

The Publishers are grateful to the following individuals, companies and picture libraries for permission to reproduce their photographs:

AKG IMAGES: 46br, 47br.
ALAMY IMAGES: 19t, 29b, 30tl, 47t.
MAK – AUSTRIAN MUSEUM OF APPLIED ARTS/CONTEMPORARY ART, VIENNA (© MAK/GEORG MAYER): 17c, 17b.

JACKET
Front – ALAMY IMAGES: Ken Walsh.
Spine – DK IMAGES: Peter Wilson b.

All other images
© DORLING KINDERSLEY
For further information see ww.DKimages.com

Price Codes are for a three-course meal per person including tax, service and half a bottle of house wine.
Cheap under €30
Moderate €30–€50
Expensive €50 or more

SPECIAL EDITIONS OF DK TRAVEL GUIDES

DK Travel Guides can be purchased in bulk quantities at discounted prices for use in promotions or as premiums. We are also able to offer special editions and personalized jackets, corporate imprints, and excerpts from all of our books, tailored specifically to meet your own needs.

To find out more, please contact:
(in the United States)
SpecialSales@dk.com
(in the UK) **Sarah.Burgess@dk.com**
(in Canada) DK Special Sales at
general@tourmaline.ca
(in Australia) **business.development@pearson.com.au**

Phrase Book

In Emergency

Help!	**Hilfe!**	**hilf**-uh
Stop!	**Halt!**	hult
Call a doctor.	**Rufen Sie einen Arzt.**	**roof**n zee ine-en **artst**
Call an ambulance.	**Rufen Sie einen Krankenwagen.**	**roof**n zee ine-er **krunk**'n-warg'n
Call the police.	**Rufen Sie die Polizei.**	**roof**n zee dee poli-**tsy**
Call the fire brigade.	**Rufen Sie die Feuerwehr.**	**roof**n zee dee **foyer**-vair
Where is /the telephone?	**Wo ist /das Telefon?**	voh ist duss **tay**-le fone?
/the nearest hospital?	**/das nächste Krankenhaus?**	duss **nayk**-ste **krunk**'n-hows?

Communication Essentials

Yes/No	**Ja/Nein**	yah/nine
Please	**Bitte**	bitter
Thank you	**Danke**	dunk-er
Excuse me	**Gestatten**	g'**shtatt**'n
Hello	**Grüss Gott**	groos got
Good bye	**Auf Wiedersehen**	owf **veed**-er-zay-ern
here/there	**hier/dort**	here/dort
What?	**Was?**	vuss?
When?	**Wann?**	vunn?
Why?	**Warum?**	var-**room**?
Where?	**Wo/Wohin?**	**Voh**/vo-**hin**?

Useful Phrases

How are you?	**Wie geht es Ihnen?**	vee **gayt** ess een'n?
Very well, thank you.	**Sehr gut, danke.**	zair goot, dunk-er
That's fine.	**Sehr gut.**	zair goot
Where is/are ...?	**Wo ist/sind...?**	voh isst/zint...?
Do you speak English?	**Sprechen Sie englisch?**	**shpresh**'n zee **eng**-glish?
I don't understand.	**Ich verstehe nicht.**	ish fair-**shtay**-er nisht
Could you speak more slowly, please?	**Bitte sprechen Sie etwas langsamer.**	bitt-er **shpresh**'n zee et-vuss **lung**-zam-er

Useful Words

big	**gross**	grohss
small	**klein**	kline
hot	**heiss**	hyce
cold	**kalt**	kult
open	**auf/offen**	owf/**off**'n
closed	**zu/geschlossen**	tsoo/g'**shloss**'n
left	**links**	links
right	**rechts**	reshts
straight on	**geradeaus**	g'**rah**-der-**owss**
entrance	**Eingang/Einfahrt**	ine-gung/**ine**-fart
exit	**Ausgang/Ausfahrt**	ows-gung/**ows**-fa
toilet	**WC/Toilette**	vay-**tsay**/toh-a-**lett**-er
free, unoccupied	**frei**	fry
free, no charge	**frei/gratis**	fry/**grar**-tiss